HAL•LEONARD
BASS
PLAY•ALONG™

AEROSMITH

VOL. 36

Cover photo courtesy of Aerosmith

ISBN 978-1-61780-320-8

HAL•LEONARD®
CORPORATION
7777 W. BLUEMOUND RD. P.O. BOX 13819 MILWAUKEE, WI 53213

In Australia Contact:
Hal Leonard Australia Pty. Ltd.
4 Lentara Court
Cheltenham, Victoria, 3192 Australia
Email: ausadmin@halleonard.com.au

Visit Hal Leonard Online at
www.halleonard.com

CONTENTS

BASS NOTATION LEGEND

Bass music can be notated two different ways: on a *musical staff,* and in *tablature*

THE MUSICAL STAFF shows pitches and rhythms and is divided by bar lines into measures. Pitches are named after the first seven letters of the alphabet.

TABLATURE graphically represents the bass fingerboard. Each horizontal line represents a string, and each number represents a fret.

3rd string, open   2nd string, 2nd fret   1st & 2nd strings open, played together

HAMMER-ON: Strike the first (lower) note with one finger, then sound the higher note (on the same string) with another finger by fretting it without picking.

PULL-OFF: Place both fingers on the notes to be sounded. Strike the first note and without picking, pull the finger off to sound the second (lower) note.

LEGATO SLIDE: Strike the first note and then slide the same fret-hand finger up or down to the second note. The second note is not struck.

SHIFT SLIDE: Same as legato slide, except the second note is struck.

TRILL: Very rapidly alternate between the notes indicated by continuously hammering on and pulling off.

TREMOLO PICKING: The note is picked as rapidly and continuously as possible.

VIBRATO: The string is vibrated by rapidly bending and releasing the note with the fretting hand.

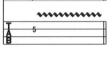

SHAKE: Using one finger, rapidly alternate between two notes on one string by sliding either a half-step above or below.

NATURAL HARMONIC: Strike the note while the fret hand lightly touches the string directly over the fret indicated.

Harm.

MUFFLED STRINGS: A percussive sound is produced by laying the fret hand across the string(s) without depressing them and striking them with the pick hand.

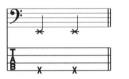

BEND: Strike the note and bend up the interval shown.

1/2

BEND AND RELEASE: Strike the note and bend up as indicated, then release back to the original note. Only the first note is struck.

1/2

RIGHT-HAND TAP: Hammer ("tap") the fret indicated with the "pick-hand" index or middle finger and pull off to the note fretted by the fret hand.

LEFT-HAND TAP: Hammer ("tap") the fret indicated with the "fret-hand" index or middle finger.

SLAP: Strike ("slap") string with right-hand thumb.

POP: Snap ("pop") string with right-hand index or middle finger.

Additional Musical Definitions

 (accent) • Accentuate note (play it louder)

 (accent) • Accentuate note with great intensity

(staccato) • Play the note short

D.S. al Coda • Go back to the sign (%), then play until the measure marked ***"To Coda"***, then skip to the section labelled ***"Coda."***

Fill • Label used to identify a brief pattern which is to be inserted into the arrangement.

• Repeat measures between signs.

1. | 2. • When a repeated section has different endings, play the first ending only the first time and the second ending only the second time.

Back in the Saddle

Words and Music by Steven Tyler and Joe Perry

Tune down 1/2 step:
(low to high) E♭-A♭-D♭-G♭

Intro
Moderate Rock ♩ = 116

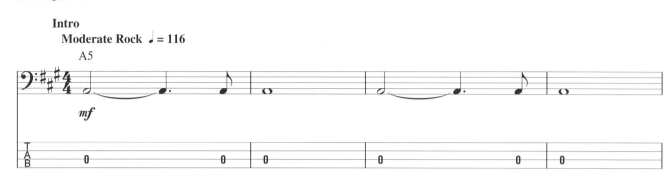

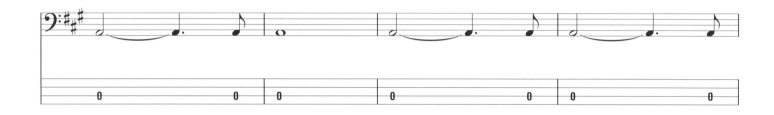

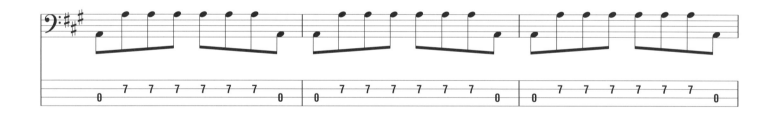

Chorus
N.C.(E5)

I'm   back,

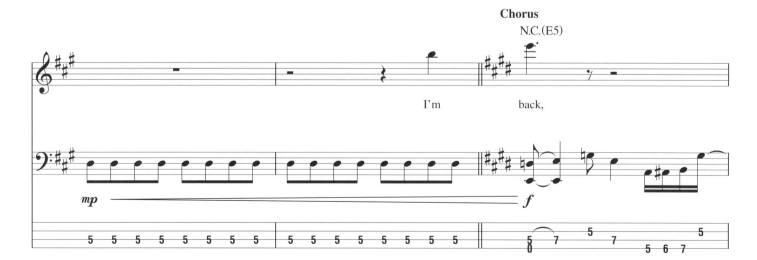

I'm back in the sad-dle a - gain. _____ I'm

back, I'm back in the sad-dle a - gain. ____

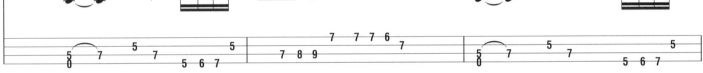

Verse

A5   D   C   D   C

_____ Rid - in' in - to town a - lone ___ by the light of the moon, ___

A5   D   C   D   C   A5   D

_____ I'm look - in' for old Su - kie Jones, ___

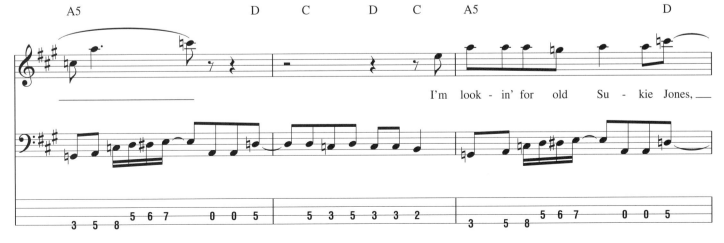

7

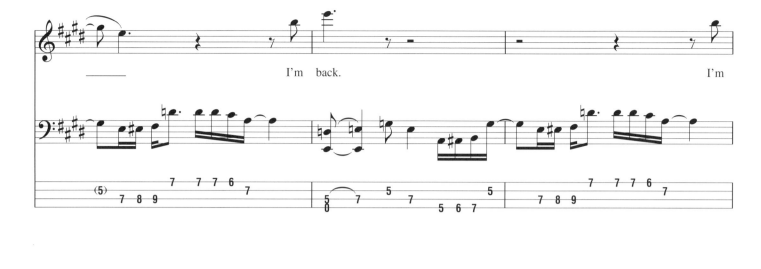

I'm back. I'm

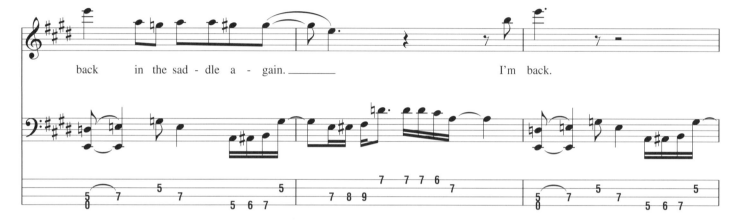

back in the sad - dle a - gain._____ I'm back.

Verse

2. Come eas - y, go eas - y, al - right ___ till the ris - in' sun. ___

I'm call - in' all the shots to - night, ___

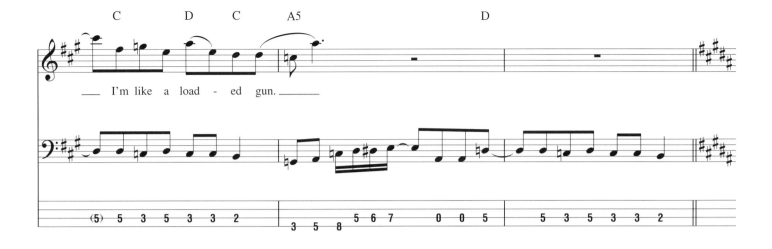

I'm like a load - ed gun.

Bridge

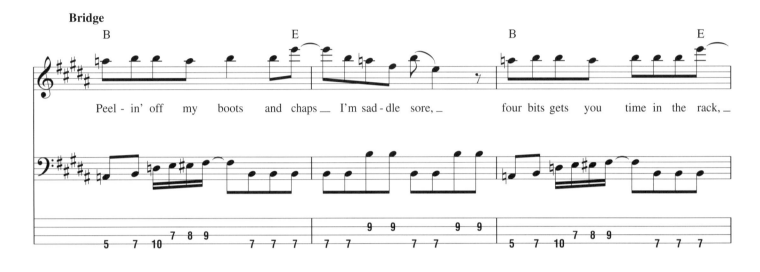

Peel - in' off my boots and chaps __ I'm sad - dle sore, __ four bits gets you time in the rack, __

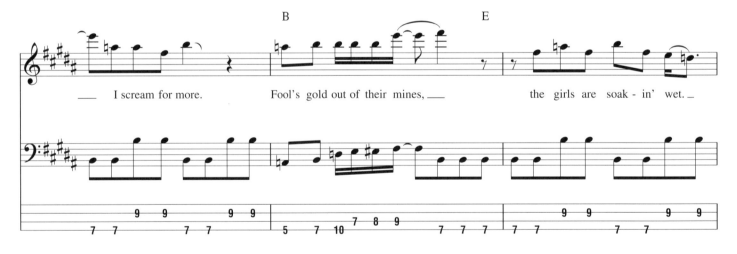

__ I scream for more. Fool's gold out of their mines, __ the girls are soak - in' wet. __

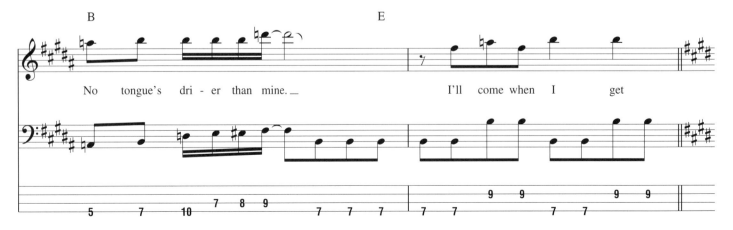

No tongue's dri - er than mine. __ I'll come when I get

Chorus

back.   I'm back in the sad-dle a - gain. ___

___   I'm back,   I'm

Bridge

back in the sad-dle a - gain. ___   I'm rid - in',

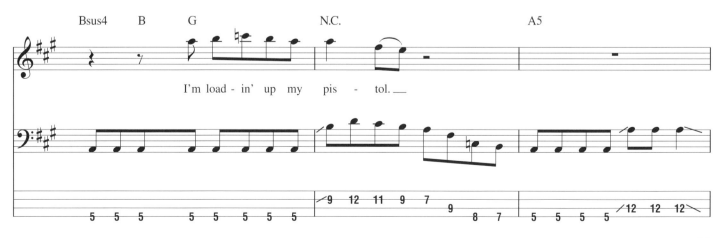

I'm load - in' up my pis - tol. ___

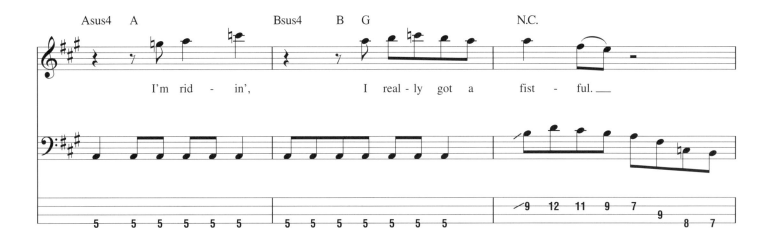

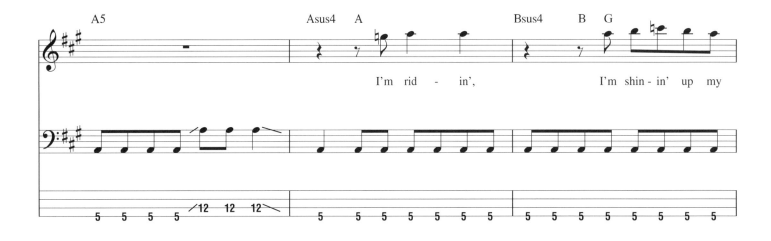

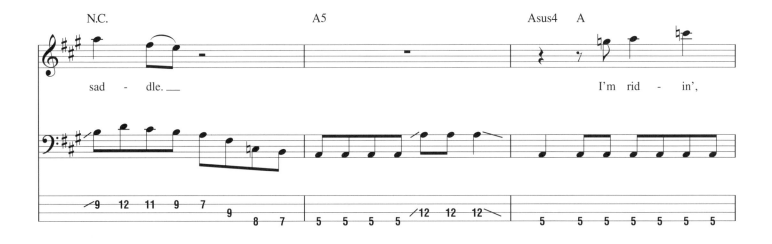

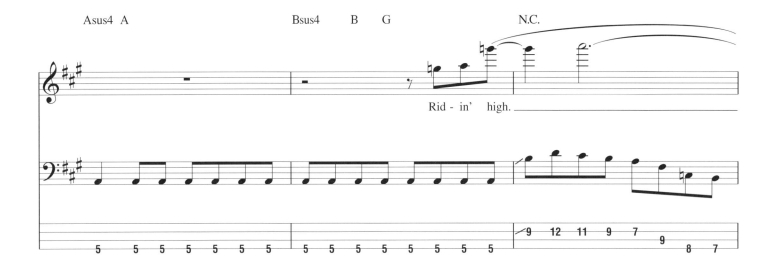

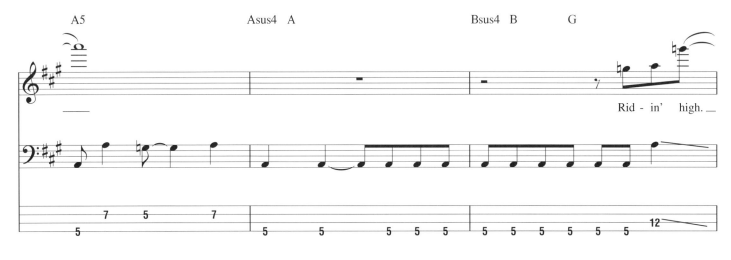

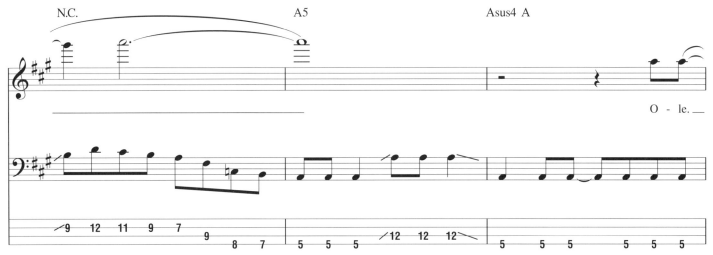

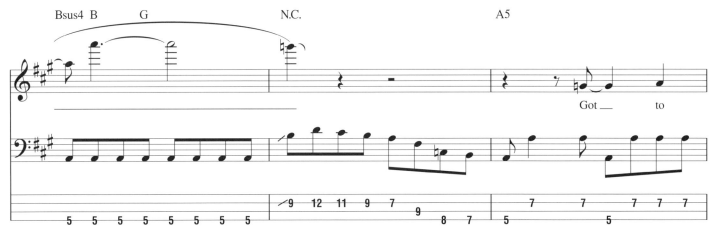

14

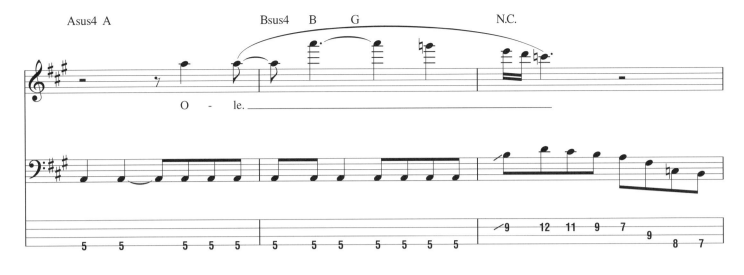

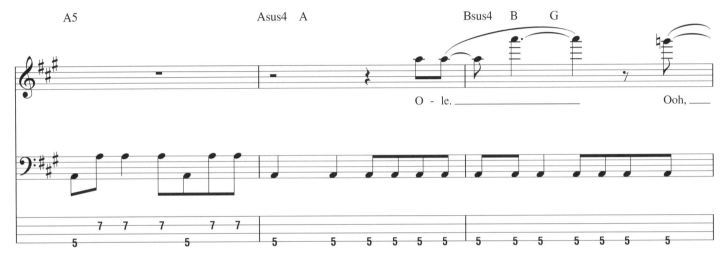

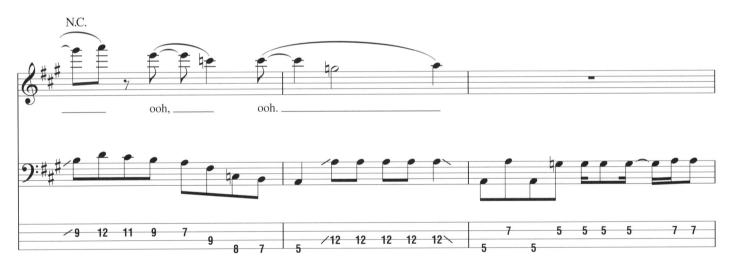

Get on! ___   Yeah! ___   Huh! ___

Draw the Line

Words and Music by Steven Tyler and Joe Perry

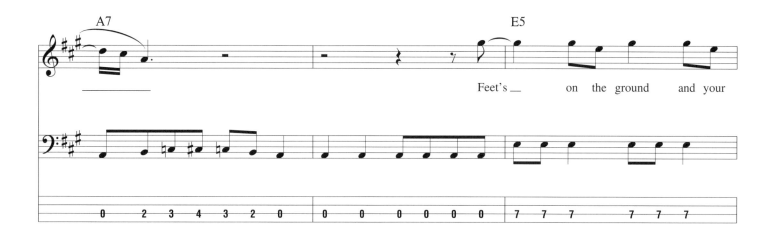

Feet's __ on the ground and your

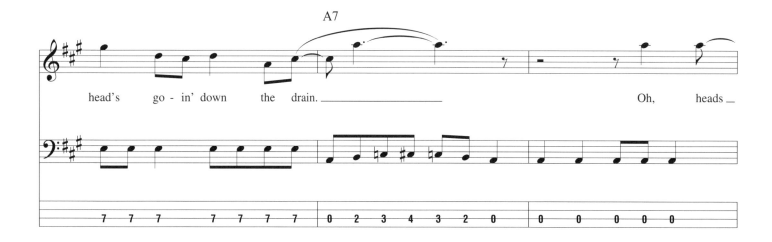

head's go - in' down the drain. _____ Oh, heads __

__ I win, tails you lose __ to the nev - er mind, _____ when to draw the line. __

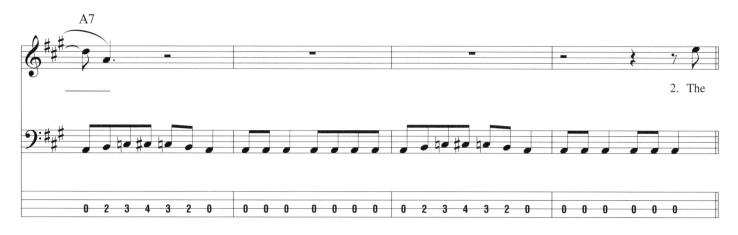

2. The

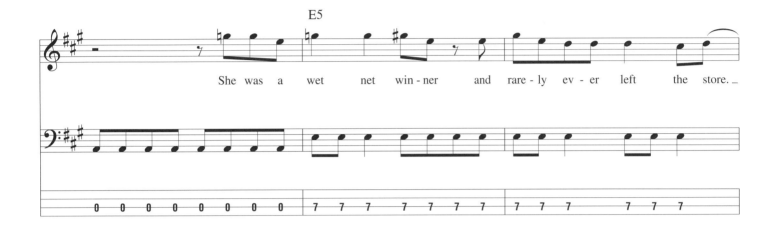

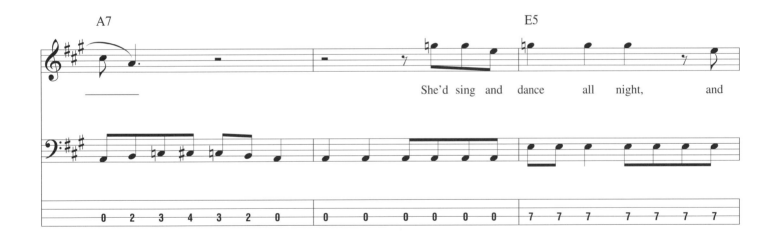

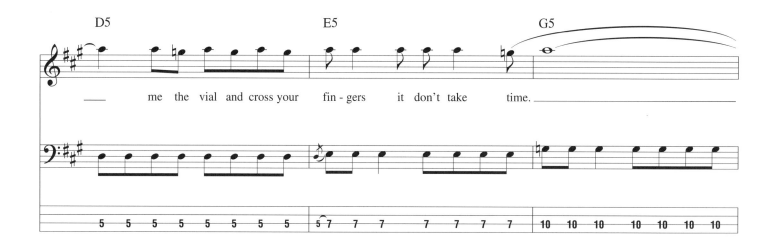

me the vial and cross your fin-gers it don't take time.

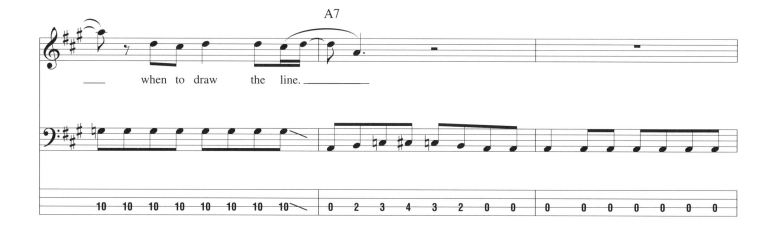

when to draw the line.

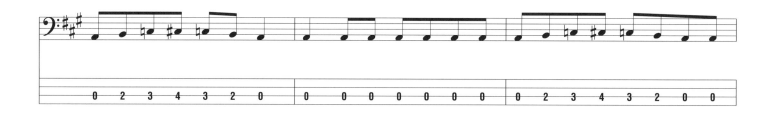

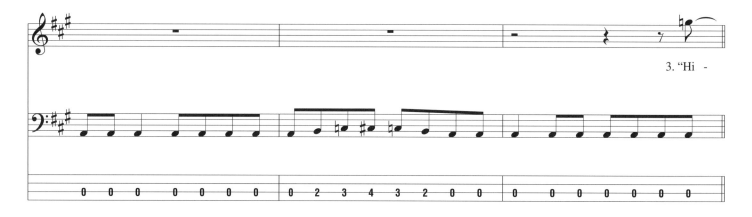

3. "Hi -

Verse

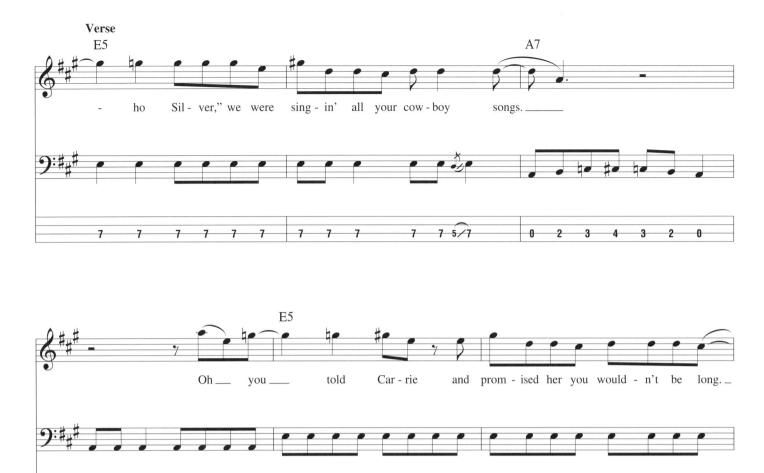

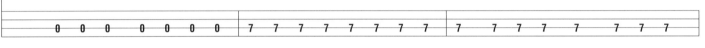

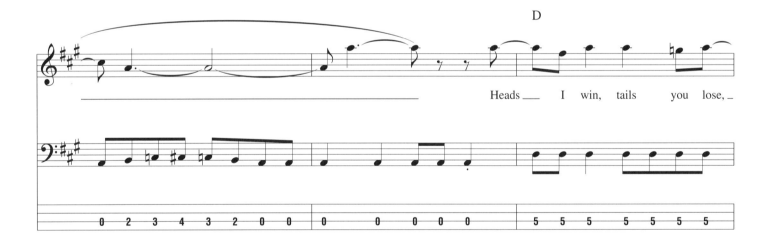

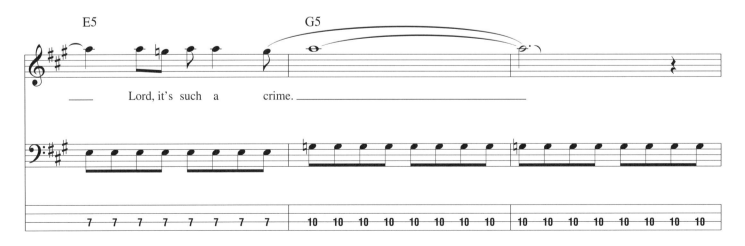

Interlude

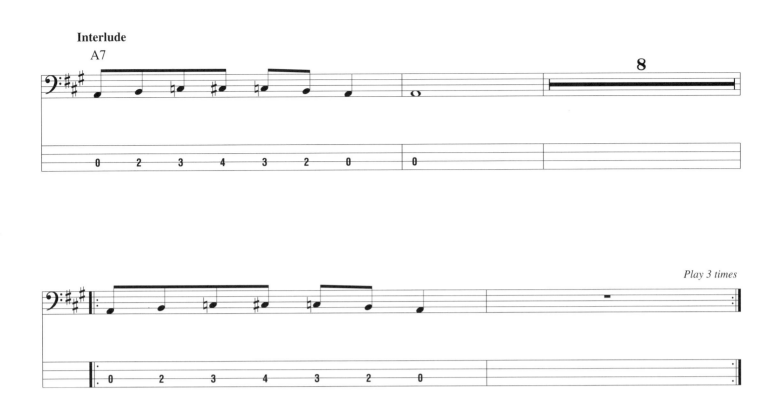

Play 3 times

Bridge

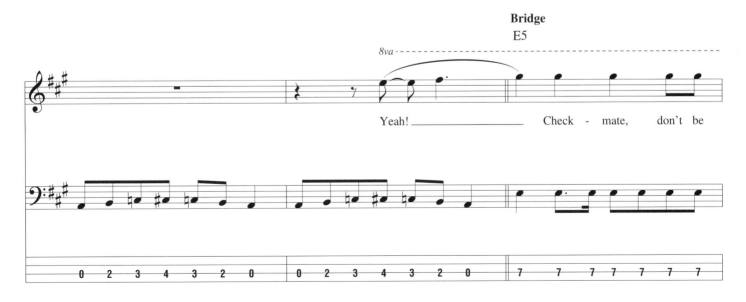

Yeah! _____ Check - mate, don't be

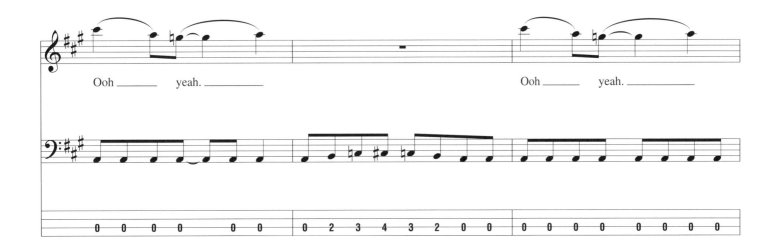

Ooh _____ yeah. _____   Ooh _____ yeah. _____

Ooh _____ yeah. _____

Repeat and fade

Ooh _____ yeah. _____

Dream On

Words and Music by Steven Tyler

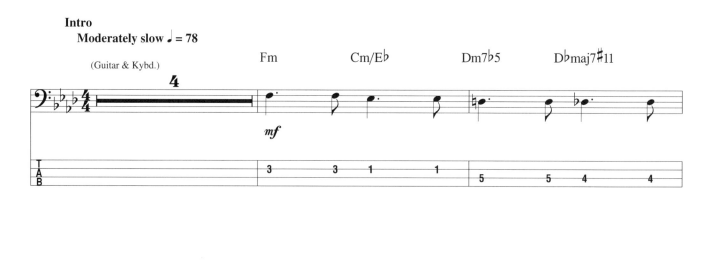

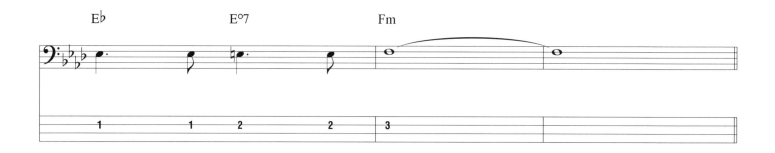

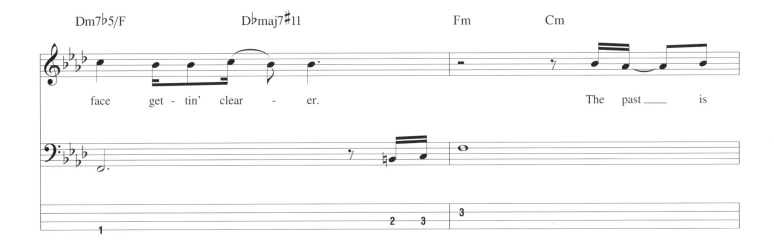

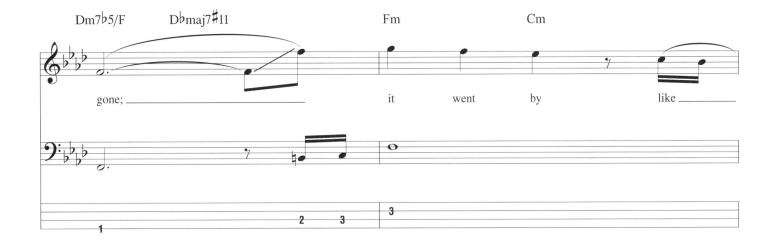

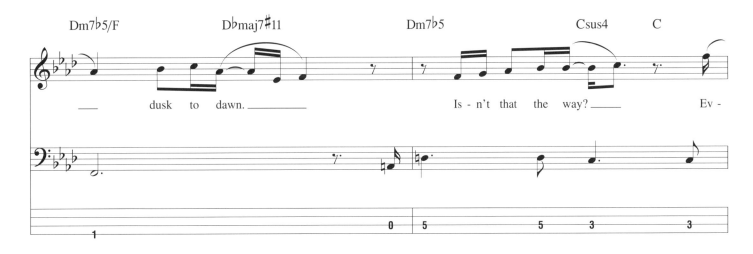

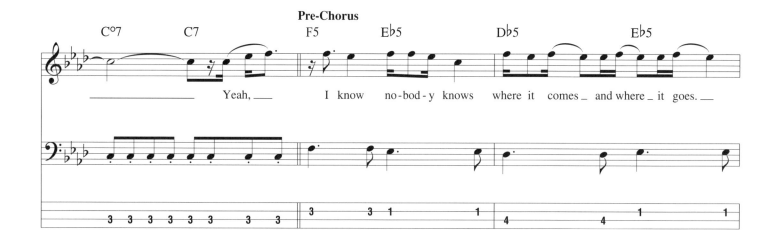

Pre-Chorus

Yeah, ___ I know no-bod-y knows where it comes ___ and where ___ it goes. ___

I know it's ev - 'ry - bod-y's sin; you've got to lose ___ to know ___ how to win. ___

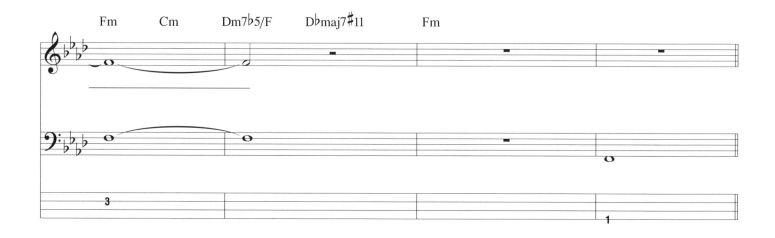

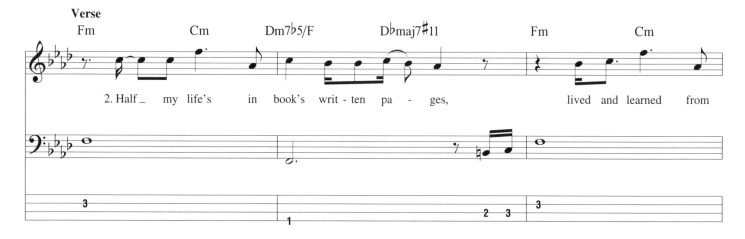

Verse

2. Half ___ my life's in book's writ-ten pa - ges, lived and learned from

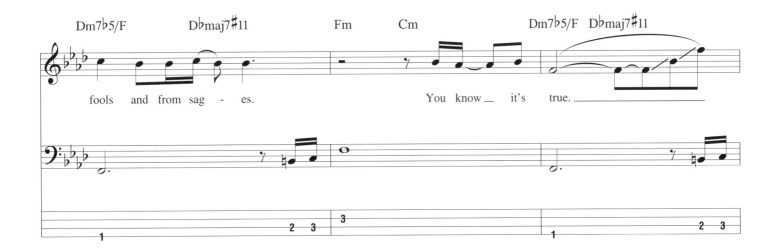

fools and from sag - es. You know __ it's true. _____

All these things __ come back to you. _____ Sing with me, sing for the years, __

Pre-Chorus

2nd time, substitute Fill 1

sing for the laugh-ter 'n' sing __ for the tears. ____ Sing __ with me if it's just for to - day, __

Fill 1

may-be to-mor-row the good Lord will take you a-way.

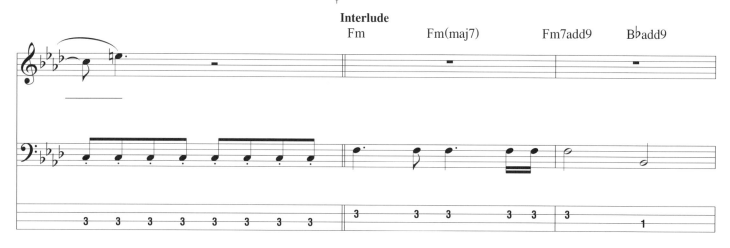

To Coda ⊕

Interlude

D.S. al Coda

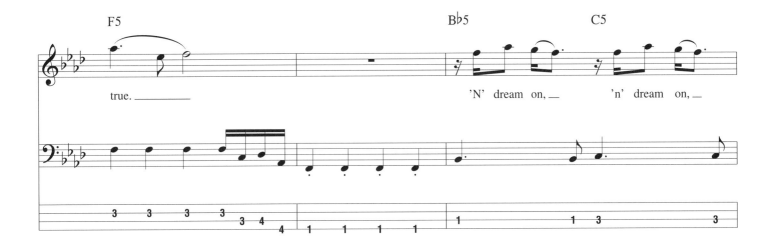

Last Child

Words and Music by Steven Tyler and Brad Whitford

Tune down 1/2 step:
(low to high) E♭-A♭-D♭-G♭-B♭-E♭

Intro
Moderately slow ♩ = 80

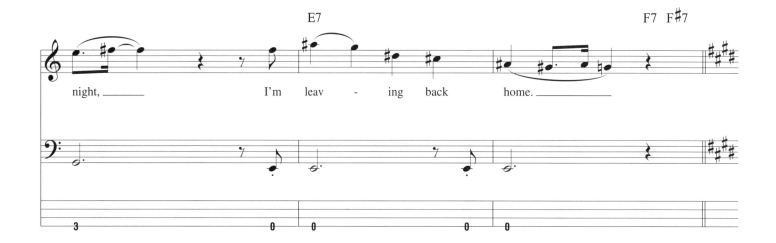

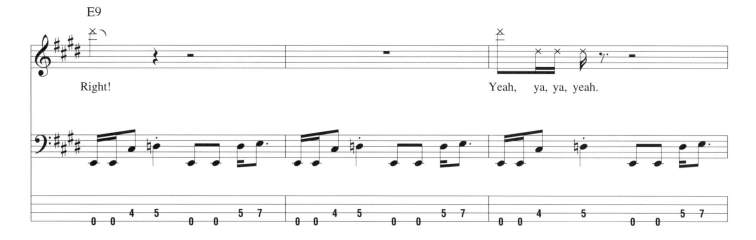

home.　　　　　　　　　　　　　　　　　　　　　　　2. Get out

Guitar Solo

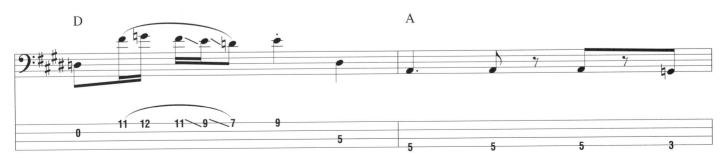

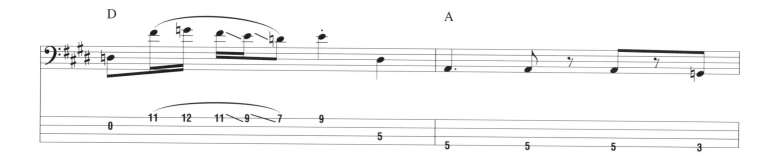

Ma - ma take me home sweet home. I was the

Outro

last child, just a punk in the streets. I was the

Additional Lyrics

2. Get out in the field, put the mule in the stable.
   Ma, she's a-cookin', put the eats on the table.
   Hate's in the city and my love's in the meadow.
   Hands on the plough and my feet's in the ghetto.

Pre-Chorus 2. Stand up, sit down, don't do nothin'.
   It ain't no good when boss man's stuffin' it down their throats
   For paper notes and their babies cry while cities lie at their feet,
   When you're rockin' the streets.

Same Old Song and Dance

Words and Music by Steven Tyler and Joe Perry

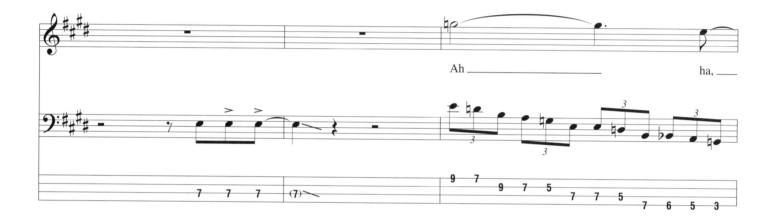

Ah _____ ha, _____

_____ right!

Verse
N.C.(E)

1. Get _____ your-self cool- er,

lay your-self low. _____ Co - in - ci - den - tal mur - der with noth - in' to show. _____ When the judge-

Chorus

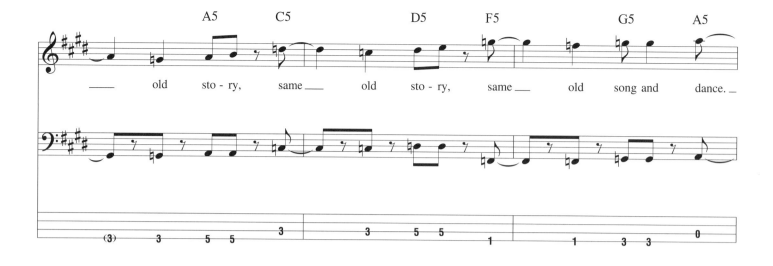

old sto - ry, same old sto - ry, same old song and dance.

Guitar Solo

To Coda ⊕

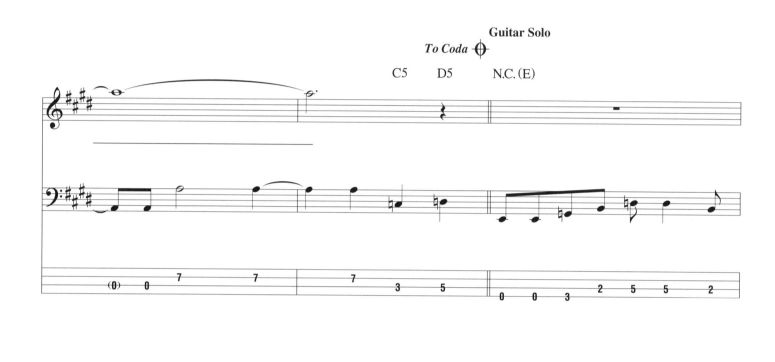

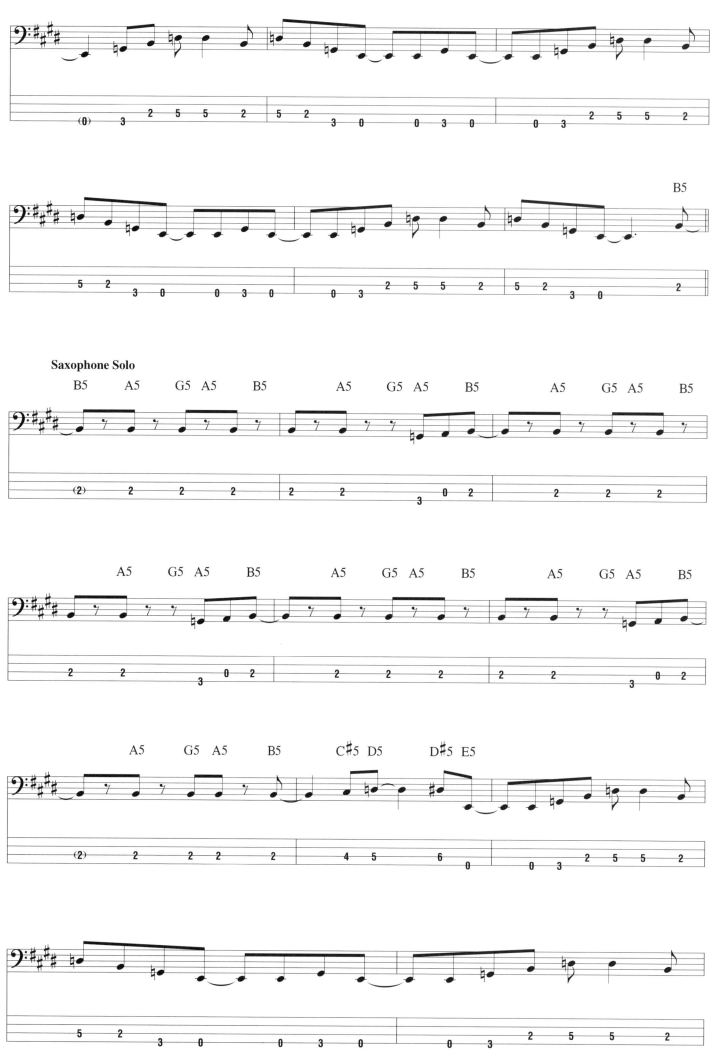

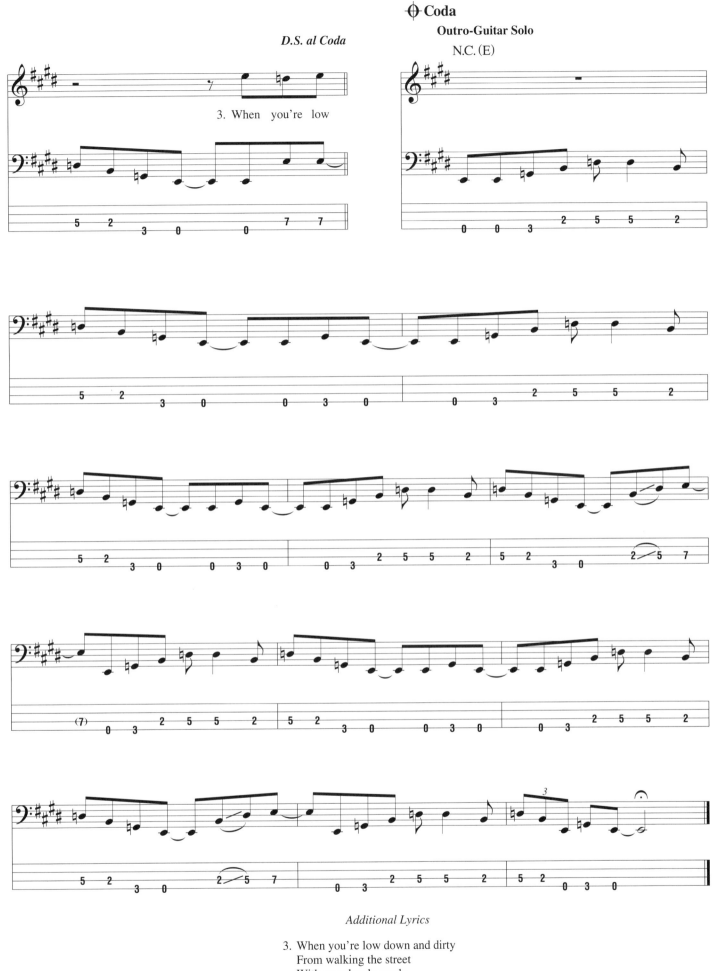

Additional Lyrics

3. When you're low down and dirty
   From walking the street
   With your hurdy gurdy,
   No one to meet.
   Say love ain't the same on the south side o' town.
   You could look, but you ain't gonna find it around.

Sweet Emotion

Words and Music by Steven Tyler and Tom Hamilton

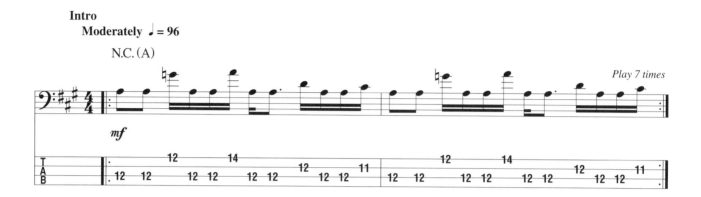

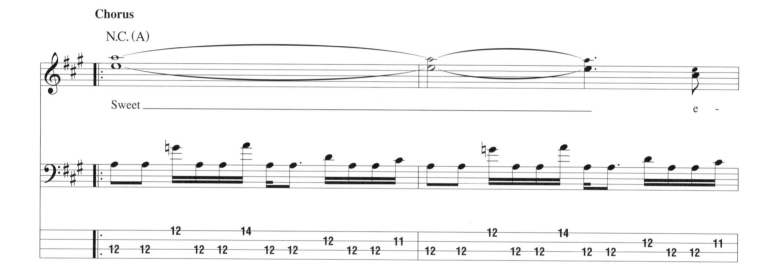

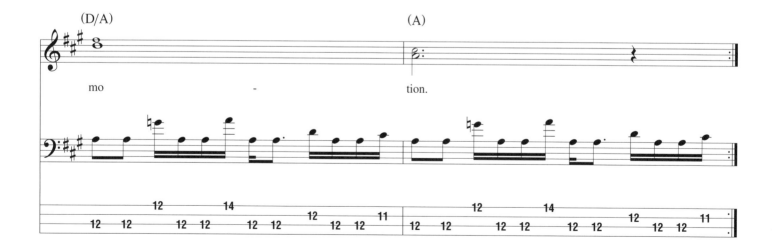

Interlude

N.C.

2. Some

Verse

2nd time, substitute Fill 1, 4 times

D   A   D   A

sweet - talk - in' ma - ma with a face like a gent
4. *See additional lyrics*

said my

Fill 1

get up and go _____ must-'ve got up and went. _ Well, I

got good news, she's a real __ good li - ar, 'cause my

back - stage boo - gie set yo' pants on fire.

Interlude

N.C.

To Coda ⊕

Chorus

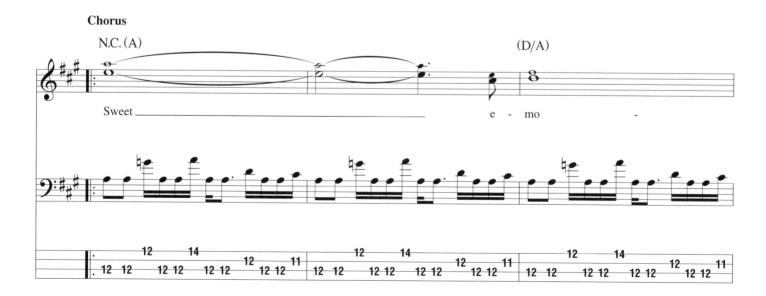

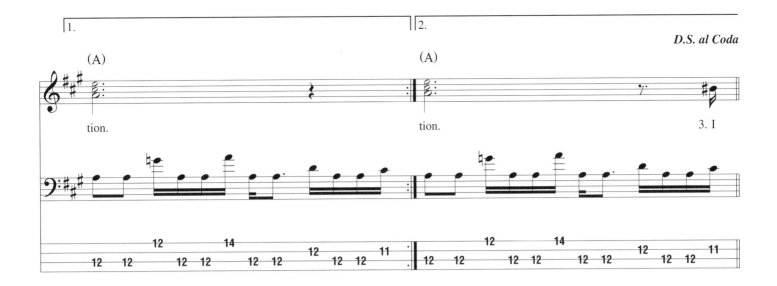

Outro

Play 12 times and fade

Additional Lyrics

3. I pulled into town in a police car;
   You daddy said I took you just a little too far.
   You're tellin' her things but your girlfriend lied;
   You can't catch me 'cause the rabbit done died.

4. Stand in front just a shakin' your ass;
   I'll take you backstage, you can drink from my glass.
   I'm talkin' 'bout somethin' you can sure understand,
   'Cause a month on the road and I'll be eatin' from your hand.

Walk This Way

Words and Music by Steven Tyler and Joe Perry

Verse

N.C. (C7)

2., 4. See - saw swing - in' with the boys in the school and your feet fly - in' up in the air, ___ I sing,

"Hey did - dle did - dle" with your kit - ty in the mid - dle of the swing like you did - n't care. ___ So I

took a big chance at the high school dance with a mis - sy who was read - y to play, ___ was a

me she was fool - in' 'cause she knew what she was do - in' { and I know'd love was here to stay when she told me to...
{ when she told me how to walk this way. She told _ me to...

Chorus

(Walk this __ way, ____   talk this __ way, ____

To Coda ⊕

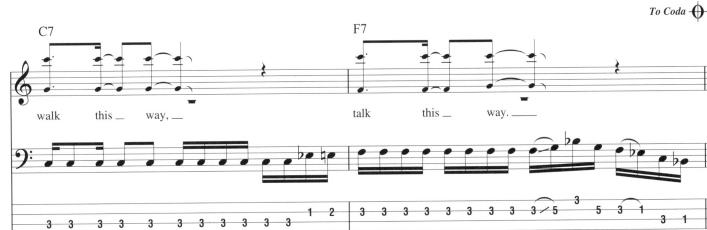

walk this __ way, ____   talk this __ way. ____

Guitar Solo
N.C. (C7)

A5

A - like   this!

Interlude

Oo.

Uh.

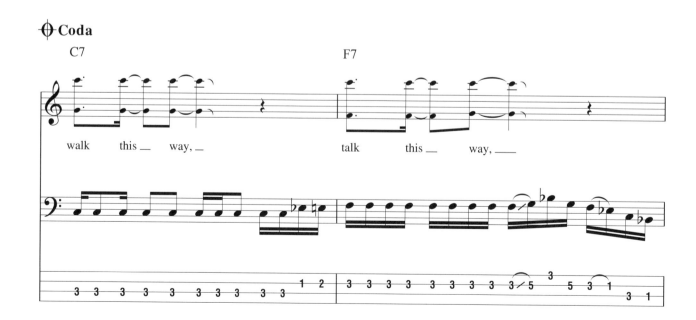

walk this ___ way, ___   talk this ___ way.) ___ Uh, just gim-me a kiss. ___

Guitar Solo

N.C. (C7)

A5

Like this!

Outro

N.C. (E5)   *Play 12 times and fade*

Additional Lyrics

3. School girl skinny with a classy kind a sassy little skirt's climbin' way up her knee,
There was three young ladies in the school gym locker when I noticed they was lookin' at me.
I was in high school loser, never made it with a lady till the boys told me somethin' I missed,
Then my next door neighbor with a daughter had a favor so I gave her just a little kiss, a like this!

Mama Kin

Words and Music by Steven Tyler

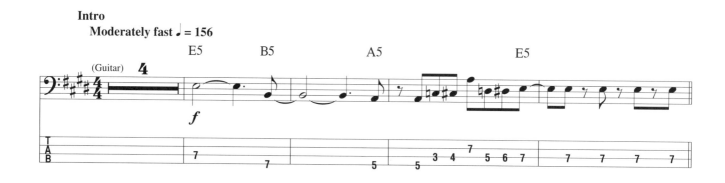

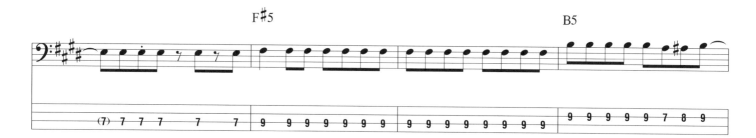

(Guitar)

E5   B5   A5   E5

Verse

E5   B5   A5   E5

1. It ain't eas - y, liv - in' like a gyp - sy.___ Tell___ ya, hon - ey, how I feel.___

I've been dream - in', float-

- in' down - stream and __ los - in' touch with all that's real.

Whole - earth lov - er, keep - in' un - der - cov - er, __ nev -

- er know - in' where ya been. _____

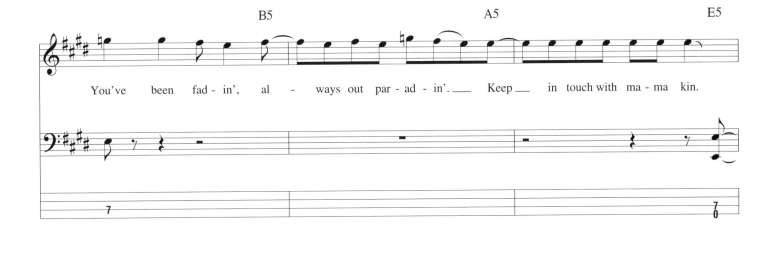

You've been fad-in', al - ways out par-ad-in'.___ Keep___ in touch with ma-ma kin.

Pre-Chorus

Well, you've al-ways got your tail on the wag, ___

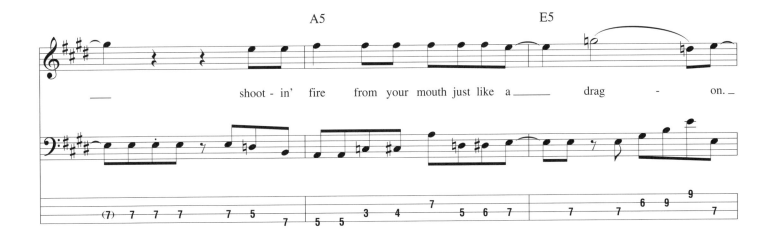

___ shoot-in' fire from your mouth just like a___ drag - on. ___

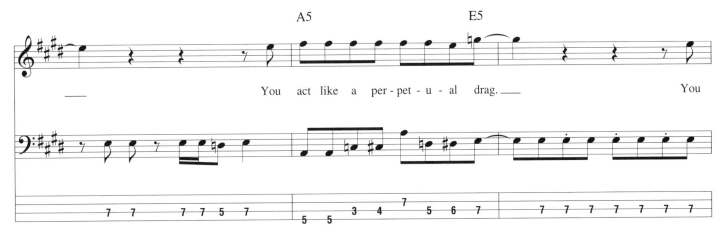

___ You act like a per-pet-u-al drag. ___ You

better check it out, 'cause some-day soon you'll have ta climb back on the

wag - on. ____

Verse

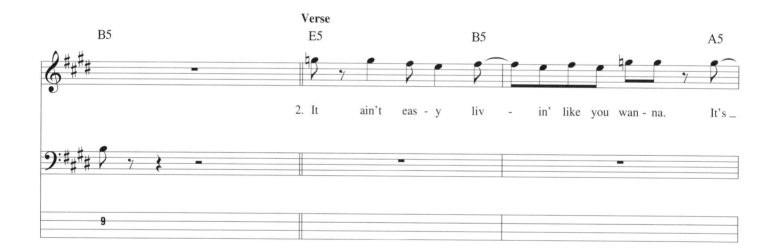

2. It ain't eas - y liv - in' like you wan - na. It's ___

___ so hard to find peace of mind. ____ Yes, it is. The

wag - on. ____

Chorus

Bass tacet

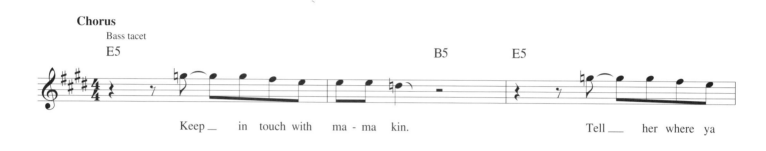

Keep __ in touch with ma - ma kin. Tell __ her where ya

gone 'n' been. Liv - in' out your fan - ta - sy.

Sleep - in' late an' smok - in' tea. Mm, hmm. Keep __ in touch with

ma - ma kin. ___ Tell ___ her where you gone 'n' been. ___

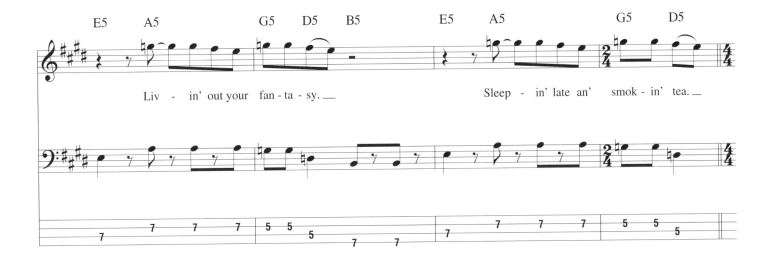

Liv - in' out your fan - ta - sy. ___ Sleep - in' late an' smok - in' tea. ___

Interlude

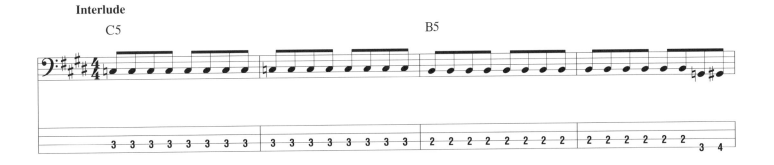

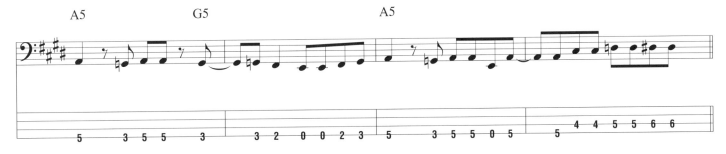

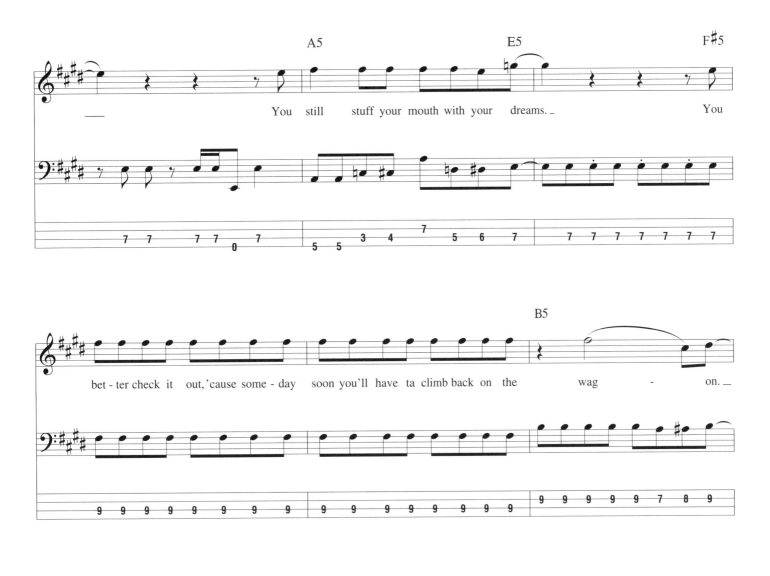

You still stuff your mouth with your dreams. ___ You

bet - ter check it out, 'cause some - day soon you'll have ta climb back on the wag - on. ___

Chorus

Bass tacet

E5   B5 E5   B5

Keep ___ in touch with ma - ma kin. Tell ___ her where ya gone 'n' been.

E5   B5 E5

Liv - in' out your fan - ta - sy. Sleep - in' late an'

smok-in' tea.   Mm, hmm.   Keep _ in touch with ma-ma kin. _   Tell _ her where you

gone 'n' been. _   Liv - in' out your fan - ta - sy. ___

Sleep - in' late an' smok - in' tea. _____

Outro

Freely

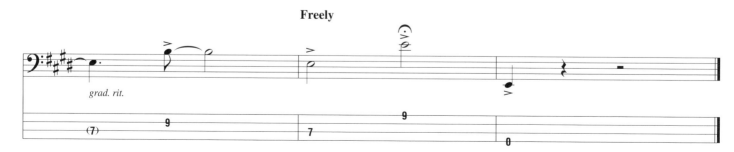

grad. rit.

BASS PLAY-ALONG

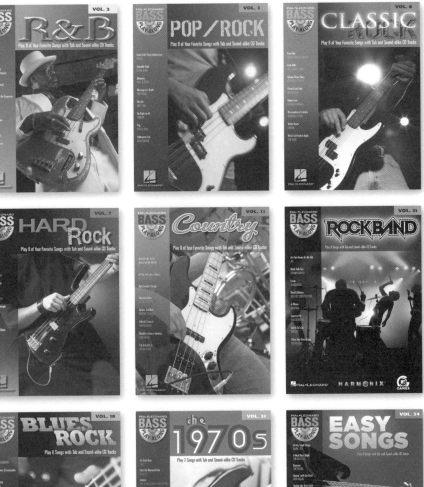

The Bass Play-Along™ Series will help you play your favorite songs quickly and easily! Just follow the tab, listen to the CD to hear how the bass should sound, and then play along using the separate backing tracks. The melody and lyrics are also included in the book in case you want to sing, or to simply help you follow along. The CD is enhanced so you can use your computer to adjust the recording to any tempo without changing pitch!

 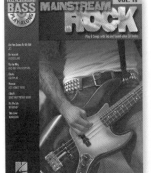  

1. Rock
00699674 Book/CD Pack..........................$12.95

2. R&B
00699675 Book/CD Pack..........................$12.95

3. Pop/Rock
00699677 Book/CD Pack..........................$12.95

4. '90s Rock
00699679 Book/CD Pack..........................$12.95

5. Funk
00699680 Book/CD Pack..........................$12.95

6. Classic Rock
00699678 Book/CD Pack..........................$12.95

7. Hard Rock
00699676 Book/CD Pack..........................$14.95

8. Punk Rock
00699813 Book/CD Pack..........................$12.95

9. Blues
00699817 Book/CD Pack..........................$12.95

10. Jimi Hendrix Smash Hits
00699815 Book/CD Pack..........................$16.95

11. Country
00699818 Book/CD Pack..........................$12.95

12. Punk Classics
00699814 Book/CD Pack..........................$12.99

13. Lennon & McCartney
00699816 Book/CD Pack..........................$14.99

14. Modern Rock
00699821 Book/CD Pack..........................$14.99

15. Mainstream Rock
00699822 Book/CD Pack..........................$14.99

16. '80s Metal
00699825 Book/CD Pack..........................$16.99

17. Pop Metal
00699826 Book/CD Pack..........................$14.99

18. Blues Rock
00699828 Book/CD Pack..........................$14.99

19. Steely Dan
00700203 Book/CD Pack..........................$16.99

20. The Police
00700270 Book/CD Pack..........................$14.99

21. Rock Band – Modern Rock
00700705 Book/CD Pack..........................$14.95

22. Rock Band – Classic Rock
00700706 Book/CD Pack..........................$14.95

**23. Pink Floyd –
Dark Side of The Moon**
00700847 Book/CD Pack..........................$14.99

24. Weezer
00700960 Book/CD Pack..........................$14.99

25. Nirvana
00701047 Book/CD Pack..........................$14.99

26. Black Sabbath
00701180 Book/CD Pack..........................$14.99

27. Kiss
00701181 Book/CD Pack..........................$14.99

31. The 1970s
00701185 Book/CD Pack..........................$14.99

33. Christmas Hits
00701197 Book/CD Pack..........................$12.99

34. Easy Songs
00701480 Book/CD Pack..........................$12.99

FOR MORE INFORMATION,
SEE YOUR LOCAL MUSIC DEALER,
OR WRITE TO:

HAL•LEONARD®
CORPORATION
7777 W. BLUEMOUND RD. P.O. BOX 13819
MILWAUKEE, WISCONSIN 53213

Visit Hal Leonard Online at **www.halleonard.com**

Prices, contents, and availability
subject to change without notice.

1010

BASS RECORDED VERSIONS

Bass Recorded Versions feature authentic transcriptions written in standard notation and tablature for bass guitar. This series features complete bass lines from the classics to contemporary superstars.

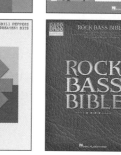
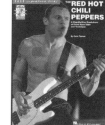

25 All-Time Rock Bass Classics
00690445 / $14.95

25 Essential Rock Bass Classics
00690210 / $15.95

Aerosmith Bass Collection
00690413 / $17.95

Best of Victor Bailey
00690718 / $19.95

Bass Tab 1990-1999
00690400 / $16.95

Bass Tab 1999-2000
00690404 / $14.95

Bass Tab White Pages
00690508 / $29.99

The Beatles Bass Lines
00690170 / $14.95

The Beatles 1962-1966
00690556 / $18.99

The Beatles 1967-1970
00690557 / $19.99

Best Bass Rock Hits
00694803 / $12.95

**Black Sabbath –
We Sold Our Soul for Rock 'N' Roll**
00660116 / $17.95

The Best of Blink 182
00690549 / $18.95

Blues Bass Classics
00690291 / $14.95

Boston Bass Collection
00690935 / $19.95

Chart Hits for Bass
00690729 / $14.95

The Best of Eric Clapton
00660187 / $19.95

Stanley Clarke Collection
00672307 / $19.95

Funk Bass Bible
00690744 / $19.95

Hard Rock Bass Bible
00690746 / $17.95

**Jimi Hendrix –
Are You Experienced?**
00690371 / $17.95

The Buddy Holly Bass Book
00660132 / $12.95

Incubus – Morning View
00690639 / $17.95

Iron Maiden Bass Anthology
00690867 / $22.99

Best of Kiss for Bass
00690080 / $19.95

**Lynyrd Skynyrd –
All-Time Greatest Hits**
00690956 / $19.99

Bob Marley Bass Collection
00690568 / $19.95

Mastodon – Crack the Skye
00691007 / $19.99

Best of Marcus Miller
00690811 / $22.99

Motown Bass Classics
00690253 / $14.95

Mudvayne – Lost & Found
00690798 / $19.95

Nirvana Bass Collection
00690066 / $19.95

No Doubt – Tragic Kingdom
00120112 / $22.95

The Offspring – Greatest Hits
00690809 / $17.95

**Jaco Pastorius –
Greatest Jazz Fusion Bass Player**
00690421 / $17.95

The Essential Jaco Pastorius
00690420 / $19.99

Pearl Jam – Ten
00694882 / $14.95

Pink Floyd – Dark Side of the Moon
00660172 / $14.95

The Best of Police
00660207 / $14.95

Pop/Rock Bass Bible
00690747 / $17.95

Queen – The Bass Collection
00690065 / $17.95

R&B Bass Bible
00690745 / $17.95

Rage Against the Machine
00690248 / $17.99

The Best of Red Hot Chili Peppers
00695285 / $24.95

**Red Hot Chili Peppers –
Blood Sugar Sex Magik**
00690064 / $19.95

Red Hot Chili Peppers – By the Way
00690585 / $19.95

**Red Hot Chili Peppers –
Californication**
00690390 / $19.95

**Red Hot Chili Peppers –
Greatest Hits**
00690675 / $18.95

**Red Hot Chili Peppers –
One Hot Minute**
00690091 / $18.95

**Red Hot Chili Peppers –
Stadium Arcadium**
00690853 / $24.95

**Red Hot Chili Peppers –
Stadium Arcadium: Deluxe Edition**
Book/2-CD Pack
00690863 / $39.95

Rock Bass Bible
00690446 / $19.95

Rolling Stones
00690256 / $16.95

Top Hits for Bass
00690677 / $14.95

**Stevie Ray Vaughan –
Lightnin' Blues 1983-1987**
00694778 / $19.95